POINTS OF VIEW

Is VIRTUAL LEARNING Good for Students?

By Layla Owens

KidHaven PUBLISHING

Published in 2023 by
KidHaven Publishing, an Imprint of Greenhaven Publishing, LLC
29 E. 21st Street
New York, NY 10010

Designer: Deanna Paternostro
Editor: Caitie McAneney

Photo credits: Cover, p. 7 insta_photos/Shutterstock.com; p. 5 fizkes/Shutterstock.com; p. 9 Anna Kraynova/Shutterstock.com; p. 11 Ekaterina Ru/Shuttersrtock.com; p. 13 Nestor Rizhniak/Shutterstock.com; p. 15 Veja/Shutterstock.com; p. 17 wavebreakmedia/Shutterstock.com; p. 19 Syda Productions/Shutterstock.com; p. 21 (notepad) ESB Professional/Shutterstock.com; p. 21 (markers) Kucher Serhii/Shutterstock.com; p. 21 (photo frame) FARBAI/iStock/Thinkstock; p. 21 (inset, left) Len44ik/Shutterstock.com; p. 21 (inset, middle) WESTOCK PRODUCTIONS/Shutterstock.com; p. 21 (inset, right) Nattapat Halpin/Shutterstock.com.

Cataloging-in-Publication Data

Names: Owens, Layla.
Title: Is virtual learning good for students? / Layla Owens.
Description: New York : KidHaven Publishing, 2023. | Series: Points of view | Includes glossary and index.
Identifiers: ISBN 9781534541931 (pbk.) | ISBN 9781534541955 (library bound) | ISBN 9781534541948 (6pack) | ISBN 9781534541962 (ebook)
Subjects: LCSH: Distance education–Computer-assisted instruction. | Web-based instruction–Juvenile literature. | Internet in education–Juvenile literature. | Education–Social aspects–Juvenile literature.
Classification: LCC LC5803.C65 O94 2023 | DDC 371.35'8–dc23

Printed in the United States of America

Some of the images in this book illustrate individuals who are models. The depictions do not imply actual situations or events.

CPSIA compliance information: Batch #CSKH23: For further information contact Greenhaven Publishing LLC, New York, New York at 1-844-317-7404.

CONTENTS

Education from a DISTANCE

Most students have done some form of virtual learning. Virtual learning, which is sometimes called distance learning, is when school takes place online. Students often do their virtual learning from home. Others have to find a place with internet **access** and the right devices, or tools. Some students learn along with their class. Others do work at different times of the day.

Many people like virtual learning. They think **technology** is going to be the key to education in the future. Others think virtual learning leaves many children—and adults—behind. Families with lower **incomes** and students with special needs may struggle.

Know the Facts!

Results from a 2020 U.S. Census Bureau study showed that people from lower-income households were less likely to have online tools for distance learning.

Devices such as laptops and tablets are important for virtual learning.

Learning During a PANDEMIC

Virtual learning has been common for college classes for many years. However, it only became common for U.S. children and teens in 2020. That year, the COVID-19 **pandemic** spread around the world. Governments and schools had to make hard choices. Most schools in the United States decided to keep students at home to stop the spread of the COVID-19 **virus**.

Because of the virus, many governments ordered people to stay home. They closed many businesses and outlawed large gatherings. They said staying apart would help keep more people safe. Virtual learning was the only way most students could learn.

Know the Facts!

About 93 percent of people in households with school-age children said that they'd done distance learning from home during the COVID-19 pandemic.

In March 2020, many schools had to rush to get their students the devices needed for distance learning.

Anywhere and ANYTIME

Many people like virtual learning because students can learn from anywhere. If there's a pandemic, they can learn from home. That can help keep them safe from getting sick. They can also learn even if school buildings are closed for bad weather.

Some students can also do their schoolwork at any time. They can wake up a little later and work later in the day or get a lot of work done in the morning and take the afternoon off. Learning from home sometimes means kids can be around their family more. Some people argue there are fewer **distractions** at home than in a busy classroom.

Know the Facts!

A July 2020 Gallup poll found that 28 percent of parents supported full-time distance learning for their children.

Some young people like distance learning because they feel more comfortable at home.

Have and HAVE NOT

Other people say that virtual learning requires the right tools, space, and support. That means it's unequal for different students. Some students don't have the space in their home to learn well. Some share a small apartment with many people. Some don't have an adult, such as a parent, available to help them use virtual learning technology. Many parents need to work.

Some students don't have the technology needed for virtual learning. Devices like laptops and tablets aren't available to all students, especially those from lower-income families. Some don't have access to the internet.

Know the Facts!

An August 2020 report from UNICEF said that at least a third of schoolchildren around the world could not participate in virtual learning.

Many students suffered without the benefits that come with in-person schooling, including meals and adult **supervision**.

You Set the PACE

Some argue that virtual learning can allow a student to learn in the best way for them. Students who can choose when they want to do schoolwork can set their own pace. They can work quickly if a lesson seems easy to them. Then, they can work on a special project or hobby.

This **flexible** schedule, or plan for the day, is a lot like many work-from-home schedules. People argue it can help students prepare for this kind of work as an adult. Some people say that it helps students learn to manage their time. This important skill can help them throughout their life.

Know the Facts!

Asynchronous learning is learning on one's own schedule, not together as a class. Students set the pace for their learning.

When students set the pace for their learning, they can take the time to find what really interests them.

Special NEEDS

Some people argue that while distance learning may work for some students, others have special needs. They might need special help from teachers to understand and complete schoolwork. Some students, such as those with **autism**, work best with the same setting and schedule every day.

Some students receive **therapy** and extra help at school. Students who struggle to speak may have speech therapy. Students who learn in different ways may get help from a special education teacher. Students who struggle with their feelings may see a school counselor. People argue that in-person school is more helpful for these students.

Know the Facts!

In the 2019–2020 school year, about 14 percent of public school students received special education services.

Some students with special needs have a hard time with virtual learning. They miss the extra help they'd get at school.

Less

BULLYING

Bullying is a big problem in schools. Some people who bully others push or hit. Some say mean words to hurt people. Others spread hurtful lies. Bullying can make students afraid to go to school. It can also make it hard for them to focus on, or pay attention to, their schoolwork.

Some people believe that distance learning cuts down on bullying. If students aren't in common places, such as a classroom or hallway, then there are fewer opportunities for in-person bullying. This can make bullied students feel safer, since they can do their schoolwork from home. It can help them focus just on schoolwork.

Know the Facts!

A 2019 study found that more than 20 percent of students report being bullied.

Most bullied students say they've been bullied in the school hallway, stairwell, or classroom.

No

COMMUNITY

Many people argue that students should be in school because of the social opportunities. Meeting, learning from, and playing with other students is an important part of a student's growth.

Being around other students also makes many kids happier. They like to spend time with their friends. They can talk to each other about things they're excited about or things they're worried about. People say that **socializing** is a big part of why going to school is good for kids. Students learn important skills, such as teamwork and sharing their feelings.

Know the Facts!

A 2020 Gallup poll found that 45 percent of parents reported their children found being separated from classmates and teachers to be a major challenge when virtual learning.

Working as a team is an important skill that students learn in school.

What's Your OPINION?

Some people feel that virtual learning is just as good as in-person learning. They point out all the cool ways that **interactive** technology can help kids get excited about learning. They talk about how technology can help students connect in new ways with their teachers and classmates. People with a different point of view feel that virtual learning means way too much screen time and not enough face-to-face time.

Virtual learning became common during the COVID-19 pandemic. That means most students today have experience with it, in one way or another. Your experience can also help shape your opinion about this issue. What do you think about virtual learning?

Know the Facts!

COVID-19 also changed the way many people work. More adults began working from home during the pandemic.

Is virtual learning good for students?

YES

- Students can often do schoolwork anywhere and anytime.
- Students can set the pace for their learning.
- Students don't have to worry about being bullied in person.
- Interactive technology creates an exciting learning experience.

NO

- Some students don't have the tools, space, and support they need for virtual learning.
- Students with special needs are sometimes left behind.
- Students aren't able to socialize.
- Students have too much screen time.

A chart can be a good tool to help you understand important debates.

GLOSSARY

access: The ability to use or have something.

autism: A disorder in which a person may have trouble communicating and socializing with others.

distraction: Something that draws a person's thoughts or attention away from something else.

flexible: Able to change.

income: The money a person gains through work.

interactive: Involving the actions or input of a user.

pandemic: An outbreak of disease that occurs over a wide geographic area and affects a great proportion of the population.

socialize: To participate in a social group.

supervision: The act of watching and directing what someone does or how something is done.

technology: A method that uses science to solve problems and the tools used to solve those problems.

therapy: A method used to treat a mental or physical health problem.

virus: A very small thing that causes disease and spreads from one person or animal to another.

For More INFORMATION

WEBSITES

Dealing with Bullies

kidshealth.org/en/kids/bullies.htmlSentence of explanation.

Some kids deal with bullying as part of in-person school. Learn how to deal with bullies with KidsHealth.

Facts About Coronavirus

kids.nationalgeographic.com/science/article/facts-about-coronavirus

Learn more about COVID-19—the virus that made virtual learning a necessity for many young people around the world.

BOOKS

Braxton, Simone. *Sometimes We Feel Lonely*. New York, NY: Cavendish Square, 2022.

Keppeler, Jill. *Pandemics: COVID-19 and Our World*. New York, NY: PowerKids Press, 2022.

Rusick, Jessica. *Understanding Autism*. Minneapolis, MN: Abdo Publishing, 2022.

Publisher's note to educators and parents: Our editors have carefully reviewed these websites to ensure that they are suitable for students. Many websites change frequently, however, and we cannot guarantee that a site's future contents will continue to meet our high standards of quality and educational value. Be advised that students should be closely supervised whenever they access the Internet.

INDEX